YOUR GUIDE TO BAR EXAM

HOW 2 STUDY LAW

PROVEN ADVICE, STUDY TIPS
AND INSIGHT FOR LAW STUDENTS

DAVID SPRINGFIELD

HOW 2 IMPROVE YOUR CONCENTRATION

HOW 2 STUDY SMARTER AND SUCCEED

HOW 2 PREPARE FOR THE BAR EXAM

Springfield EXamPRESS

www.how2studylaw.com

Springfield Exam Press, Sacramento, CA 95825
© 2005 by David Springfield
All rights reserved. Published 2005
First edition published 2005
Printed in the United States of America

ISBN-13: 978-0-9765507-0-9
ISBN-10: 0-9765507-0-9

How 2 Study Law.—1st ed.
Author: David Springfield
Editor & co-author: Engelbert Goethals

www.how2studylaw.com

TABLE OF CONTENTS

introductory note—study with passion | v

before getting started | 1

how 2 essentials—
time and energy management | 8

study phase I—course work | 21

study phase II—exam preparation | 40

essays, MBEs, and performance exams 40

how I prepared for the California Bar Exam and passed | 54

appendix a—helpful websites | 64

appendix b—united states state bar organizations | 69

appendix c—law schools | 71

INTRODUCTORY NOTE
study with passion

At the beginning of our first year of law school, Dean Michael Clancey of Northwestern California University School of Law (www.nwculaw.edu), told us, a group of first year law students, that if there's one thing he recommends it is to be *passionate about the law*. Dean Clancey is absolutely right: Your passion, your enthusiasm, is the first and most important key to success in the study of law. Without that passion, you won't have the drive, the motivation, or energy to do well. Passion helps you find the minutes, hours, and days in your week to devote to the study of law and the determination to persevere.

To be successful, however, you also need to understand **how to study and what to do**. It's all too easy to get lost studying minute details before getting the necessary overview. In my first year of law school, I spent weeks being fascinated with reading the casebooks, only to find that I couldn't recite a single rule of law, legal principle, or the required elements of a tort or crime. I was simply too busy being absorbed by it all.

The following structured approach works! No matter what law school you attend, this is an intensely **practical** study method to help you succeed on law school examinations and then to reach your ultimate goal: to pass the Bar Examination.

[signature]

HOW❷TIP

study with passion

"If you are resolutely determined to make a lawyer of yourself, the thing is more than half done already."

Abraham Lincoln

BEFORE GETTING STARTED

The prerequisites may appear to be matters of common sense, but if you're going to study law, you will soon learn that common sense is not so common!

get the basics right

1. State Bar Requirements
2. Law School Requirements
3. Financial Requirements

state bar requirements

To practice law in any state or jurisdiction, you must be licensed or admitted to the bar under the rules established by the jurisdiction's highest court. Federal courts and administrative agencies set their own qualifications, but most require you to be licensed in the state in which the federal court or agency is located.

All states require you to pass a written bar examination and a written ethics examination as well. You can obtain your Juris Doctor (J.D.) degree without taking the state bar examination. But if it is your goal to practice law, you will need to become fully familiar with and satisfy all the state bar requirements of the state where you intend to get licensed.

You have to meet certain educational requirements and register with the State Bar organization of your state; find out how, when, and where to file bar exam applications, and how to register for the MPRE (Multistate Professional Responsibility Examination) as well as to fulfill the moral character determination requirements, which usually consist of providing detailed background information showing you have the requisite good moral character to be an attorney.

I suggest that you refer to **Appendix B** for the websites of all the United States state bar organizations.

Then print out all of the membership requirements, cross off the ones you have met, calendar what you still have to accomplish, and then **DO IT**.

california state bar
no actual college required

In California, even if you have no college credits, it is possible to fulfill your educational requirements by meeting certain test scores on a test called CLEP (College-Level Examination Program) administered by the College Board: www.collegeboard.com. The CLEP, which offers the opportunity to demonstrate college-level achievement through a program of exams in undergraduate college courses, is administered regularly in test centers around the country. You will need to pass three tests with scores in a percentile specified by the California State Bar. You can repeat these tests until you pass. For more details, see www.calbar.ca.gov.

Some law schools will require college degrees, while others accept a certain number of college credits or CLEP scores without the degree. Similarly, some schools require LSAT testing with certain minimum scores, others don't. See **Appendix C** for a list of all law schools.

In most large bookstores, you can purchase books that help you score high on the CLEP or LSAT tests. These books are also available on the Internet at www.amazon.com, www.barnesandnoble.com, or at legal bookstores, such as www.americaslegalbookstore.com.

law school requirements

Every law school has its own requirements as to admission, classes, attendance, exam taking, grading, law review, etc. If you intend to apply for admission to a law school that's in high demand, apply to more than one, since competition is intense. Once accepted, you have to become fully familiar with your law school's educational requirements, test score requirements, programs, curriculum, and other options such as law review.

Formal education requirements generally demand a college degree, but in California you may satisfy these requirements by the CLEP tests mentioned above for most non-ABA (American Bar Association) approved schools.

There are three-year (full time) and four-year (part time/correspondence) programs that culminate in the granting of the Juris Doctor degree (J.D.). Four-year programs include night school and correspondence and/or online law schools. There are ABA approved schools, State Bar accredited law schools, correspondence law schools, and non-accredited law schools.

Note that "non-traditional" study methods may restrict your ability to later take the bar or practice law in other jurisdictions.

Carefully examine the law school you intend to apply for as well as the percentage of students passing the bar from that school. If you study law through a non-ABA approved law school, make sure that the state bar for the state where you wish to practice will accept your degree for purposes of meeting its eligibility requirements.

For California, obtain a copy of the booklet called *Rules Regulating Accreditation of Law Schools in California*. Send your request to:

Department of Educational Standards
Office of Admissions
The State Bar of California
180 Howard Street
San Francisco, CA 94105

Night law school or correspondence law school in most states is a four-year program as opposed to a traditional three-year full time schedule, but for those of us who can't afford to take three years off to dedicate ourselves full time to law study, this may well be the only reasonable option.

create a master schedule

After fulfilling your preliminary educational requirements and filing your law school application(s), create a Master Schedule with the appropriate due dates. Check off your accomplishments!

sample master schedule

DATE	TO DO	COMPLETED
August 1, 2006 etc......................	Register with State Bar Midterm Exams (Year I) Application Baby Bar (if required) Final Exams (Year I) Baby Bar Examination (California only) Midterm Exams (Year II) Final Exams (Year II) Midterm Exams (Year III) Final Exams (Year III) Application and MPRE Exam Moral Character Determination Application Midterm Exams (Year IV) Final Exams (Year IV) Bar Examination	...........✓........... ....

what will you learn in law school?

There are, besides the traditionally required courses such as contracts, torts, criminal law, civil procedure, constitutional law, property, etc., many optional classes on interesting subjects, such as civil rights law, family law, taxation, international studies, European Union law, and classes teaching basic and advanced skills in legal writing, legal research, and trial advocacy. Pay close attention to all your state's Bar Examination subjects if it is your goal to become a practicing attorney.

A good book that gives a taste of what you may expect to do and learn in law school is *One L* by best-selling author Scott Turow. A good movie with the same focus is *The Paper Chase*, directed by James Bridges, about a group of Harvard freshmen in law school whose first year's grades are a matter of life and death.

I worked as an investigator and paralegal throughout law school and knew what areas of law I wanted to specialize in. Your interests will determine your focus. For me, law study by correspondence was the only feasible method. I was forced early-on to find and apply the most effective study methods. I'm sharing them with you in this guide.

your interests will determine your focus

california bar exam subjects

- torts (including products liability)
- contracts/UCC (uniform commercial code)
- remedies
- criminal law
- criminal procedure
- evidence
- civil procedure
- real property
- constitutional law
- corporations
- wills
- trusts
- community property
- professional responsibility

Effective July 2007 the scope of the California Bar Examination will change as follows:
- The subject currently titled "Corporations" will be renamed "Business Associations" and the scope of the topics tested in Business Associations will include those topics currently tested in Corporations, partnerships of all forms, limited liability entities, related agency principles, and uniform acts.
- The scope of the subject titled "Civil Procedure" will include the California Code of Civil Procedure.
- The scope of the subject titled "Evidence" will include the California Code of Evidence.

financial requirements

Attending law school is a significant financial investment. Expect some stress while you juggle making a living and obtaining an education. But try to make sure from the start that financial concerns won't cause excess worry.

California is one of three states that permit law study by correspondence, which is among the least costly options. For a listing of correspondence law schools in California, see www.calbar.gov. It's possible to obtain your law degree and pass the bar examination for $12,000 to $15,000, including materials.

Working full time while studying law is a realistic endeavor if you're willing to make the right sacrifices and are disciplined. Remember Benjamin Franklin's sage advise: "*What maintains one vice would bring up two children.*" (...and still pay for law school.)

For information on financial aid, loan packages, scholarships, and various other sources for funding law school, go to a helpful section of www.findlaw.com for law students: "Pre-Law Resources: Financing Law School" (www.stu.findlaw.com/prelaw/finance.html).

HOW☉TIP

> remember Benjamin Franklin's sage advice:
> *"What maintains one vice would bring up two children."*
>
> (...and still pay for law school)

introduction

The following ideas and principles are not only mine. That's why they are valuable. They are simply the essence of what I've learned from the experience, wisdom, and knowledge of others: professors, friends, lawyers, and colleagues.

Some ideas may appear breathtakingly simple. That doesn't mean that they are not effective. Simplify your problems—you probably have enough of them!

planning

Benjamin Franklin said: *"If you fail to prepare, you're preparing to fail."*

HOW❷TIP

> ## realizing your goals builds
> ## self-confidence and satisfaction

The more you realize your goals, the more your self-confidence will grow. This is an important principle. Planning and scheduling help you to define and achieve your goals. That's why planning and scheduling are so important. Analyze the future and envision the best way to reach your goal. One way is through the preparation of your optimized daily study schedule, discussed in the next chapters.

Not reaching your goals, on the other hand, will undermine your self-confidence and won't give you any satisfaction. But at the same time, planning is a learning process, and you should use your 'failures' as challenges and incentives to plan better and study harder next time. You can only reach your goals by pushing your limits. Sometimes that means going *beyond* your limits.

You need to know where you want to go, or you're surely not going to get there. Probably, if you're reading this now, it's your goal to complete law school and successfully pass the bar examination. No matter how much or how little time you have left before the bar exam, planning with these methods will make your study more effective.

> ## thoughtful planning helps define your goals
> ## plan your work—then, work your plan

Plan in a practical way. Don't set unrealistic goals that defeat your intention to succeed. A common pitfall is that we take on more than we can accomplish such that we unwittingly set up to sabotage our dreams of law school success and of passing the bar exam. Then, after failing to pass a hurdle, we often rationalize unreasonably as to how and why we didn't make it. Don't self-destruct: make your first goals deliberately small, so you will achieve them successfully. Then make your goals gradually bigger.

You will see that if you plan your school year, with detailed goals for the months and weeks, then your days will go well because they are part of a comprehensive plan. You will get more done, even when things don't go according to schedule. Remember, the more detailed your planning, the better.

Planning must become a habit. Plan in as much detail as reasonably possible. As planning becomes more of a habit, studying will naturally become a more spontaneous, relaxed, and focused process.

work with a specific goal

Work with a specific goal. Erasmus wrote: "*If you keep thinking about what you want to do or what you hope will happen, you don't do it and it won't happen.*" A goal is not just a wish or a dream but a specific result achieved through action.

Know exactly why you're doing something. It's useful to ask yourself the question: "What is my ultimate educational or professional goal?" Answering this question for yourself affects your productivity, because the better you know your goal, the better the chance of reaching it. Know why you're doing something, in small and large things; understand the goals of the course, the lecturer, the case you're briefing, etc. If you know why you're doing something, if you understand the meaning of it and don't see it as meaningless, everything will go easier.

your goal: pass the bar examination

Have the specific goal to do one thing well in your life: pass the bar examination. This large goal can be divided into lots of smaller goals. Your planning deliberately breaks this large goal up into its constituent parts: yearly, monthly, weekly, and daily goals. Keep your eye firmly on your large goal. This will remind you that time flies.

Share your large goal with some supportive friends or family members. You're not alone! People love to help and support you. Later these same people will ask you for free legal advice.

ask yourself the right questions

A common misconception is that simply working hard, i.e., spending many hours on legal materials, will get you where you want to go. Wrong! Don't assume that studying hard automatically gives the best results. Productivity research has shown repeatedly that working long hours doesn't necessarily result in increased productivity. Similarly, the amount of hours spent with law school material is largely irrelevant.

You have to study **smart**. You will only find the right study methods and techniques by **asking** yourself the right questions, **finding** the correct answers, and then **putting** these into practice! This doesn't mean that you don't need to spend a very considerable amount of time with your studies—*you do*—but it has to be part of a balanced, intelligently strategized study program—not mindless, low-level brain activity.

Ask Yourself the Right Questions:

- What does my day look like?
- How do I use my time?
- Do I actually waste time?
- Do I sleep too much?
- Do I have concentration problems?
- Do I read efficiently?
- Can I profit from a speed-reading course?
- Can I improve my note taking?
- Are my studies suffering from my study environment?
- Am I using the best course books and materials I can get?
- Do I have a plan for memorizing key materials?

This guide focuses on these questions in detail, and more...

Observe and verify what works and what doesn't. By observing what personal habits further your studies and which ones hinder your study results, you will fine-tune your study habits. Don't assume you already know them. Giving a second thought to study habits is almost always best. By assuming you already know, you miss the chance to improve your study methods. Remember, wishful thinking is the downfall of scholarship.

Once you're on the right track, keep improving your methods through active and consistent questioning. What worked for one moment or situation may not work for another moment or situation. For example, listening to introductory tapes may be great to obtain an overview of a course, but it can be a waste of time during your final exam preparation.

Similarly, what works for one person doesn't always work for another person. A good example is the "study group" or the group bar exam preparation classes. It may be great for some but a total waste of time for others.

Find out how **you** learn best. Be flexible in your thinking. Flexibility means intelligence.

a note about changing habits

Mark Twain wrote: *"To break a habit, you must not fling it out of the window, but walk it down the stairs, one step at the time."* In other words, when changing habits, change them gradually. Don't bite off more than you can chew.

Take the example of sleeping habits. Many of us can do with less sleep, but you need to give the body time to adapt. Instead of suddenly sleeping two hours less, gradually get up ten minutes earlier each day until you have reached your goal. If you need more time for your law study, this is one way to get it.

study schedule and daily schedule

Here the main rule is: *Know what you are doing!* That is, be aware of how you spend your time. People who deliver optimal results know exactly what they are doing and why they are doing it. Just look at any great athlete—their training schedules, diets, etc., are scientifically calculated to deliver optimal results. Of course, the opposite is equally true. People who aren't aware of how they are spending their time don't deliver. So the best advice with regards to your daily study schedule is: *Know what you are doing!*

HOW❷TIP

> ## know what you are doing
> ## at all times and why

Here is an exercise that will put you on the right track. For two weeks, try writing down on a notepad throughout your day everything you do and when you do it. Be precise! Take this notepad with you everywhere you go. This exercise alone will already increase your efficiency and productivity 20% to 100%, simply because it makes you aware of how you're really spending (read: *wasting*) your time! You will see, perhaps painfully but clearly, what works, and what doesn't.

Here is an example of what your notes may look like:

<table>
<tr><td colspan="2">_Daily Time Management Notes_</td></tr>
<tr><td>8:00 AM:</td><td>Get up, shower</td></tr>
<tr><td>8:55 AM:</td><td>Breakfast</td></tr>
<tr><td>9:15 AM:</td><td>Study</td></tr>
<tr><td>9:45 AM:</td><td>Coffee break/newspaper</td></tr>
<tr><td>11:15 AM:</td><td>Study</td></tr>
<tr><td>12:00 Noon:</td><td>Lunch</td></tr>
<tr><td>1:00 to 5:00 PM:</td><td>Nap</td></tr>
<tr><td>5:00 to 6:00 PM:</td><td>Dinner</td></tr>
<tr><td>6:00 to 10:00 PM:</td><td>TV / visit to Starbucks</td></tr>
<tr><td>10:00 to 10:15 PM:</td><td>Frantic study for exam</td></tr>
<tr><td colspan="2">_(Help! I'm never going to make it!)_</td></tr>
</table>

As you can see in the foregoing example, you may have the feeling you spent the entire morning studying, but in fact you only studied for 1 hour and 15 minutes.

optimize your daily study schedule

For most students it is best to study for at least a few hours in the morning, immediately after getting up. Don't wait—you will have plenty of opportunity to get deviated the rest of the day. Your brain is fresh from the night's rest, so this is a good time for memorizing definitions, elements, mnemonics, etc., for a short period such as 15 or 20 minutes. It also warms you up for study later in the day. Doing the daily 15-20 minutes of memorization is tremendously effective.

Whether you're a morning or evening person, the early hours are best suited for studying, in particular for memorization.

Based on this, the optimized daily study schedule is more or less as follows:

OPTIMIZED Daily Study Schedule

6:29 AM: Get up, splash some water on your face
6:30 AM: Study—start with memorization
7:15 AM: Some exercise or meditation, shower
7:30 AM: Study
8:15 AM: Breakfast
8:30 AM: Study
9:15 AM: Run, Workout, etc.
          (Depending on other requirements)

The key here is that by 9:00 a.m. you have already accomplished some serious studying and your day has just started. You will feel more "on-top of things" so to speak. Compare that to the previous schedule. Make every minute count.

Why does the early bird catch the worm? There's no fully satisfactory explanation. Some scientists claim this depends on the very nature of our biological clock. Others say that people dream more during the morning hours. Since dreaming tends to make the mind tired, people who rise late will be mentally less rested and deliver less. But whatever the cause, the proven fact is that by following the Optimized Daily Study Schedule, study results improve greatly.

In general, the optimized daily study schedule will be similar for most law students. Of course, personal variations are possible. If you're a night owl, you're not going to change what works for you—just adapt the above productivity model and optimize the use of your time.

Finally, don't study if you're too exhausted. Get some rest instead! If you're tired because of bad diet, excessive consumption of alcohol, etc., then you know what to do! Get in shape physically as well as mentally.

Alcohol impairs cognitive function as well as memory by inhibiting the transfer of information to your long-term memory!

don't drink while learning— it literally dulls the brain

how to achieve consistency

Perhaps not surprisingly, it has been demonstrated that regular and consistent daily study is better than the occasional, intense, daylong or all-night-long sessions. You're better able to memorize terms and definitions by taking 10 minutes 6 days per week than by trying to memorize the same in one hour all at once.

So study consistently, following the same schedule every day to avoid cramming. Studying a few hours each day is much more effective than studying a whole day during the weekend. Reward yourself for staying on schedule. Muster all the will power you need to keep on target. After some weeks, you will feel great simply by keeping your goal. This will propel you to continue studying consistently.

Still, do what you have to do. From time to time, I've had such a busy schedule I could only study on weekends. Don't feel guilty about not being perfectly "on schedule." Remain flexible and always study with a positive attitude. Some all-day or all-night projects are useful because they stretch your thinking about how much you can do.

study time intervals

Psychologists have demonstrated that the best period for mental efforts such as studying is a 45 to 50 minute segment followed by a short break. This is true, although with exam preparation, it's important to stretch the duration of sustained intellectual efforts to at least two to three hours. Why? To get ready for real exam conditions.

Find **your** best study time interval. Some athletes are naturally better short-distance runners, others are better long-distance runners.

My (little) brother Peter just successfully ran the Carmel International Marathon. He told me that training for this grueling event (including the infamous Hurricane Point—a steep climb over several miles in the middle of the course) didn't consist of running 26.2-mile-marathons everyday, but running repeatedly variable *shorter* distances (5-8-10 miles, etc.) to get in shape, train endurance, and build enough strength to be ready for the final run. His marathon *interval* training method reminded me an awful lot of my bar exam preparation.

HOW❂TIP

the important thing is to finish successfully
you don't need to win the race

For daily study, a great method is to study for 45 minutes, followed by 15 minutes of working out, doing dishes, raking the lawn, or some social activity. Remember, before you were a law student, you were a relatively normal human being—try to keep up that pretense! The 15-minute interval refreshes the brain and aids in retention of material. After 15 minutes—get back into it. Try it!

how to improve concentration

The most common misconception about concentration is that it can't be learned or improved. Most people think that their ability to concentrate is good, ordinary, or bad compared to others, and that's where their thinking stops. This is simply not true.

Concentration, the mental ability to control and give your attention to a given subject, can be developed through training. The more intelligent your training program, the better the results. **The key to remember is that you <u>can</u> learn to control your attention and, therefore, improve your concentration.**

To study well, you have to learn how to *intentionally* focus and hold your attention. While studying, your attention isn't automatically attracted and captivated as it is while watching a good movie. Rather, you have to deliberately bring your attention to the material you're studying. This is the very essence of concentration. In George Orwell's words: *"To see what is in front of one's nose needs a constant struggle."* That's why you have to strengthen your focus; otherwise a thousand and one things will distract you.

HOW❂TIP

you can learn to control your attention

So how do you learn it? The brain is like any other muscle: by making intensive use of it through focused practice you can strengthen it.

The great thing is that <u>every</u> situation in your life can help improve your concentration. Just try to focus on what you're doing, and stop trying to do many things at once. **FOCUS!** Simple everyday situations like breakfast, washing dishes, etc., can all become useful exercises in concentration.

Take the example of breakfast. Try to have your next breakfast with as much intentional concentration as possible, from beginning to end. When preparing your cup of coffee or tea, keep your mind to it. Give it your best attention, moment after moment, step by step. When drinking your coffee, really taste and enjoy every sip of it, and don't allow your mind to drift away from the situation.

Keep your mind, as much as you can, focused on having your cup of coffee. This is extraordinarily hard to do. If you're truly honest, you will admit that you're constantly being deviated and that you drift off into daydreaming, or you find yourself thinking about what you're going to do tomorrow. But the more you practice, the better you will be able to focus. This is the quality attention you have to bring to your studies.

Apply the same exercise to other daily tasks and chores (e.g., listening to the daily news). The main thing is to focus on the task at hand. Concentrate on what you're doing in the moment—*moment after moment*—relaxed, but with attention. You will also observe that your ability to focus will fluctuate from day to day. Yet, with sustained practice, you will improve your ability to consciously control your attention. You may be surprised to find out that after some practice you will be able to control your attention much more than you expected.

Holding your attention is an effort, but when practiced correctly and consistently, it also creates an intense feeling of relaxation and relief. And, your coffee will have never tasted better!

As mentioned earlier, it is good to alternate a period of intense study with a period of physical exercise or other activity. It will help concentration and will improve your efficiency. This method has stood the test of time. In Zen monasteries, for example, it is common practice to alternate long sessions of meditation with periods of intense physical labor to create a healthy balance between body and mind. To pass the bar, you must become a samurai warrior of your own mind...

concentration and relaxation

You know it is easy to control yourself and stay relaxed in familiar, everyday situations. However, in new and intense situations, people tend to get nervous. So what exactly are nervousness and anxiety? Behind nervousness and anxiety is fear of what the results or consequences might be if something goes wrong.

Often, people fail exams, not because they are incompetent, but because they're overwhelmed by fearful thoughts and worries that take most of their attention.

The solution has already been given. Nervousness and anxiety are due to a lack of focus, i.e. insufficient ability to focus and concentrate. An exam situation is one of these new and intense situations where you lose your normal attention if it's not sufficiently developed. The solution: Learn to hold your attention on what is right there at the moment in front of you (hint: it's probably something you studied).

These are the keys to relaxed exam taking: a carefully planned and detailed study program, an optimized daily schedule, regular and consistent study with maximum concentration, and sufficient exercise, meditation or sport.

HOW❷TIP

practice daily relaxed concentration

on the day of examination

Especially on the day before the examination and the day of the examination, focus as much as possible on the task at hand, whether it is having breakfast, taking a shower, or reviewing some final study material. What if you have doubts? Doubt is a universal phenomenon. Everyone suffers from it at times. Don't take it personally. For some, it helps to firmly say to themselves: "Just get over it!"— Others will need to remind themselves that they have done all they could, practice positive thinking and some deep breathing…

Whatever your mindset at the time of examination, try to put out optimal effort at exam time. Tell yourself to give it all you've got.

optimize your study environment

Find or create a good study space: a space where you have good lighting, minimal distractions, your law school books, your *Black's Law Dictionary* (an absolute must), and your computer readily accessible. You're going to do a lot of writing and legal research so a good computer or laptop will be very handy.

You need a quiet space where you can focus and work uninterrupted by people, noise, ringing telephones, etc. Do everything you can to have a *dedicated* desk for your studies.

Items to have readily available:
- Pens
- Post-it stickers
- Yellow highlighters
- No. 2 pencils
- Pencil sharpener
- Note paper
- Ruler
- Paperclips, stapler, tape dispenser
- Make sure to have good Internet access for your online legal research

dry erase board

I'm a big fan of dry erase boards because they give an "at-a-glance" overview and are great for making notes. I have one in my study and one in my office. Dry erase boards are also great for keeping score of how much you've done. Keeping score is one of the best motivators.

Buy one or more at the hardware store or office supply store. For $15 you can have a prominent space of 4 x 6 feet where you can write critically important study notes.

three phases of law study

Your law studies can be divided into *three* main phases.

During the first phase, you will learn the substance of each law school course (e.g., Contracts, Criminal Law, Civil Procedure). You will study to develop comprehensive understanding of the subjects and memorize the important concepts, definitions, and rules of law of each course.

During the *second phase*, you will practice taking actual exams. You will write essays, time them, and have them graded; you will practice under real-life exam conditions.

The first and second phases lead to the *third phase*: passing the examinations.

the three phases

LEARN the course
PRACTICE exam taking
PASS the exams

Obviously, you need to start with the first phase wherein you master the substance and develop knowledge and understanding of each course's subject matter. This beginning, learning the course, is the most important part of the work because you need a strong foundation. Without mastery of the subject matter, no clever exam writing can cover up ignorance of the substantive rules of law.

The key is to not get completely lost in the first phase of studying the substantive material. Don't wait until you know it all—you won't. *Realize that practicing exam taking—the second phase—is what ultimately counts.* **Spend at least one third of the time, or more, practicing for exams.** This may seem like a lot, but by practicing exam taking, you will see the gaps in your knowledge that will need to be filled with substantive study, so the second phase actually complements the first phase.

There are plenty of horror stories of students from top law schools who believed they could simply dispense with preparation for the bar altogether since they were so terribly intelligent. They were, but failed their bar examinations miserably nevertheless.

The key is to start practicing exam taking as soon as you have a basic mastery of your course. A few months into the course is usually a good time because now you have some law under your belt.

HOW☻TIP

don't wait too long before practicing exam taking

Of course, after just a few months, you won't know the course's subject matter to perfection, but start practicing exam taking anyway. Many very intelligent people fail in law school. Their perfectionist nature won't allow them to move on to the practice of exam taking. They are proof that perfect is the enemy of good. Learn from their mistake.

remember: perfect is the enemy of good

look up legalese and difficult words

Glossing over unknown words is dangerous as this breeds misunderstanding. During my studies, I would almost daily come across a word, term, or Latin phrase that I didn't know or understand. I made a firm rule to stop reading and look up these words or terms in my dictionary or legal dictionary (having both handy is a <u>must</u>), and then I wrote the word and its meaning down on a 5 x 7 index card. I kept lots of them around and reviewed them regularly.

sample index card

Impractical—not sensible or prudent, unwise to implement
Impracticable—not capable of being carried out or put into practice

Usage: A plan may be <u>impractical</u> if it involves undue cost or effort but may still not be <u>impracticable</u>.

Make a firm commitment to building your vocabulary. As a lawyer, and therefore as a law student, you have to be very precise. Your understanding of difficult words and concepts must become a tool for you, rather than a stumbling block from the lack thereof.

never, ever, gloss over a word you do not understand—it breeds misunderstanding

memorize definitions

The ability to define basic legal concepts and list their elements needs to become second nature. There's no shortcut: *they have to be memorized.* It builds confidence to have your definitions "hardwired" in your memory. It's best to do 10–15 minutes per day first thing in the morning when still fresh. Or have a family member or friend test you. My father, Herman, was absolutely merciless testing me several weeks before the Baby Bar—such dedicated help is a great motivator.

If you find a better definition, change it in your definition list. Learn one good definition, not three, for the same term.

Add to your list of definitions the rules of law and all mnemonics you want to recall during the course. In law school, I created lists of definitions for each course. You can easily create your own lists; just buy a small notebook for each course and start writing a definition on each page. The extra space on the page leaves room for changes and further refinements you want to memorize.

HOW☻TIP

make a master list of definitions, mnemonics, and rules you need to memorize for each course

and review regularly

mnemonics

Mnemonics are memory aids. You can use mnemonics to recall lists or elements or a sequence of matters to discuss on an exam.

For example: use a short sentence such as "**I P**ut **F**ive **B**ucks **D**own" to recall the elements to be discussed in order to obtain remedies in equity, such as an injunction: **I**nadequacy of legal remedy; **P**roperty interest; **F**easibility of enforcement; **B**alancing of interest; **D**amages peculiar to equity.

The word mnemonics is derived from the name of the Greek goddess of memory, *Mnemosyne*. Add your favorite mnemonics to your lists of definitions. Make your own and then you will never forget them. Some people benefit from lots of mnemonics; others simply have a few key mnemonics for each course.

flowcharts

Sometimes it is handy to make a flowchart or other chart that will aid you in retention of materials. The flowchart can be a useful visual aid assisting your memory. Whatever you need to commit to memory, put it in the same notebook of definitions and mnemonics. That way you memorize all you have to memorize for each course.

total recall—how to hardwire your memory

Memory fades because of insufficient nourishment or training. In that sense, memory is just like any other muscle in the human body. You can't expect to gain great abdominal muscles simply by doing one thousand sit-ups once in your life—you need to work at it. This means a routine of abdominal exercise with an optimal rest in between workouts.

Similarly, psychological studies have shown that the development of a strong memory or ability to recall is accomplished by a training program that has a routine for memorization.

For recall, use whatever you need to memorize and practice that use at regular intervals. You will need to be highly disciplined to achieve optimal results, especially since there are such large amounts of information for the study of law that need to be recalled at will.

After your initial study of the subject, write out your list of items to memorize. Then calendar a Total Recall Memory Schedule. (This can be done in the daily morning session of your study time).

total recall memorization chart

Create List of Definitions	Day 1
First Recall Memorization Session	Day 2
Second Recall Memorization Session	After 1 Week
Third Recall Memorization Session	After 2 Weeks
Fourth Recall Memorization Session	After 1 Month
Fifth Recall Memorization Session	After 3 Months
Sixth Recall Memorization Session	After 6 Months
Seventh Recall Memorization Session	After 9 Months
Eighth Recall Memorization Session	After 1 Year

make an outline for each course

Create a one-page outline for each course. This one-page outline lists the topics and subtopics you need to master in that course.

A one-page outline is extremely helpful. Reviewing it frequently and writing it out regularly will "hardwire" the various chapters of the course and will prove very useful during exams. *Remember: every essay exam and every multi-state question (MBE multiple choice question) will **always** fall under one or more of these general topics in the course.* The outline forms an ideal way to sort and organize those topics.

For example:

torts outline

Intentional Torts

Assault
Battery
False Imprisonment
Intentional Infliction of
    Emotional Distress
Trespass to Land
Trespass to Chattel
Conversion

Defenses to Intentional Torts

Self Defense
Defense of Others
Defense of Property
Recovery of Property
Shopkeeper's Rule
Crime Prevention/Arrest
Necessity (public/private)
Consent

Negligence

Definition and Elements:

Duty
Breach
Causation (Actual & Proximate)
Damages
*Defenses

Landowner Liability Standards
Res Ipsa Loquitur-Theory
Negligent Infliction of
    Emotional Distress

Strict Liability

Animals
Conditions on Land
Unreasonably Dangerous
    Activities
Strict Products Liability
*Defenses

Product Liability

Theories
Elements Restatement Second
    Section 402A
*Defenses

Miscellaneous Torts

Defamation
Invasion of Privacy
Nuisance (public/private)
Litigation Torts
Malicious Prosecution/Abuse of
    Process
Fraud/Deceit/Negligent
    Misrepresentation
Business Torts

Other Tort Concepts

Vicarious Liability
Joint and Several Liability
Indemnification/Contribution

how to create a one-page outline

You can create the one-page outline from the table of contents of your casebook or from a commercial outline of a course. Or go directly to the State Bar website and find out what the bar examiners consider the important parts of the course you're taking.

The one-page outline can later be refined by adding in required elements, some rules or code sections you want to include in your overall overview of the course.

Don't think you're wasting time creating, redrafting, and writing out the one-page outline. Before delving into a casebook, it is good practice to have the outline ready next to your book. Time spent reviewing the table of contents is not only time well spent, it may well be the most important time spent on the casebook.

By having the one-page outline committed to memory, as well as your definitions, you will have a knowledge base from which to draw when issues are being raised in an exam. It functions as a checklist: quickly go through the one-page outline in your mind when writing an essay to see if you missed any issues.

study the casebook

The great Persian Sufi poet, Rumi, said: *"The aim of a book is to instruct, but you can also use it as a pillow."* Certainly casebooks are useful for both.

A casebook is a collection of abbreviated case decisions and legal opinions. It illustrates how the court decided a case or how an appellate court or Supreme Court determined legal issues on appeal and made law. The opinions of the judge, justice, or magistrate will decide, affirm, or reverse a disputed legal question and provide the rationale therefore. This is known as the case-law method.

Casebooks also serve as a starting point for classroom instruction and discussion. After the case summary, the author of the casebook may pose hypothetical questions and notes for further thinking and discussion.

Don't waste time underlining and highlighting each and every page into impressionistic paintings of red, yellow, pink, blue, and orange.

A casebook isn't for memorization but for understanding legal reasoning and principles, understanding the few truly-need-to-know important cases in each course (such as *Palsgraf v. Long Island Railroad* in Torts; *Hadley v. Baxendale* in Contracts, etc.) and getting the big picture and overview.

Exceptions are Constitutional Law and Criminal Procedure courses, where virtually all cases are important because they are decisions of the highest court in the country, the United States Supreme Court.

Additionally, by working through the casebooks, you can see how almost each issue has many layers of differentiation. However, this isn't the time to get overly absorbed by minutiae. While going through the casebook, frequently refer back to your outline.

HOW❷TIP

CASEBOOKS

Before going through a section in the casebook, take a few minutes and ask questions that you would like to see answered on the topic.

Write your questions down.

Then read *actively: try to find answers to your questions.*

Some legal concepts take more time to master. For example, Proximate Cause in *Torts*, Res Judicata and Collateral Estoppel in *Civil Procedure*, or Estates in Land and Future Interests in *Real Property*—these are complex areas that need to be "digested." This is done by reviewing them repeatedly and by active attempts to grasp the concepts, preferably with outside materials, such as a hornbook (an authoritative work that sets forth the "black letter law" in the course) or other explanatory material.

Mark those important areas that you want to review later with a post-it or book-mark. Try to understand the most general principle first, distill it down to a rule of law you can memorize, and keep reviewing it, gradually expanding your knowledge and ability to define concepts in the area at issue. Above all, *don't get lost. Stay focused on the Outline and see where the ideas fit in.*

speed-reading

Why speed-reading? As soon as you get your first casebooks, you'll see that you have lots and lots of reading to do. You can spend 10 minutes per page or 1 minute per page—obviously, in a 1000-page casebook that makes a tremendous time difference (you can't make up for all this time by simply sleeping less, as discussed earlier).

There are many excellent books about speed-reading on the market. Speed-reading doesn't mean you gloss over, skim, or skip through the text. With proper speed-reading, you still read <u>every</u> word; however, you minimize habits that slow down the intake of the material, such as verbalizing (lip-reading) each word on the page. The great thing about speed-reading is that it will also increase your comprehension. It's all about concentration.

Most speed-reading or speed-learning methods will have you first go through books several times very quickly before reading each page. By spending this time getting to know the contents a little and seeing the skeleton of the work, you will have a better overall picture and overview.

Studying, adopting, and practicing a speed-reading method will vastly increase your reading speed and understanding capacity. With a tremendous amount of material to absorb, even a small increase in your reading speed and comprehension will pay off. Just be careful and don't sacrifice comprehension for speed.

As stated before, some concepts will take time and require repeated reading. Casebooks aren't novels, they are heavy-duty reading. Most are well in excess of 1000 pages. By adopting a speed-reading method, your time spent on casebooks can be cut in half or better *without* sacrificing comprehension.

When I started reading casebooks, I found them incredibly fascinating and was reading very slowly because I tried to memorize everything while reading. Timing myself, I realized each page took 10 minutes or more. At that slow speed I would still be reading Prosser's *Torts* today. After learning and then applying a speed-reading method, I was able to literally increase my reading speed at least 10 times, saving lots of time.

note taking

What about taking notes? Is it useful to take notes as you plow through the casebooks or attend lectures? Yes, but be judicious about it. How often do you take notes only to never review them? Don't be afraid to *read* only or in a lecture *listen* only. If you take notes, use a visual method whenever possible, such as drafting a graph or chart, so you have a visual overview rather than merely handwritten notes.

It's useful to memorize definitions and lists of elements early-on in the coursework, before in-depth study of the casebooks, because they make the material fall into place, thus eliminating the need for massive note taking. Don't reinvent the wheel. You will find definitions in your commercial outlines and a thoughtful analysis of elements in the hornbooks.

Also, with the speed-reading method discussed above, you will read over the material a number of times. The first reading is meant to give you a rough overview. This isn't the time to take notes yet.

brief the required cases

Your law school may require you to brief cases. A case brief is a synopsis of the main points determined in the case. Some law schools require you to brief all cases in the case books, others only require a certain number of cases to be briefed.

Tab with a post-it (sticky note) the cases to be briefed before going through the casebook. See where they fit in the outline. Case briefing, making an abbreviated summary of the main points of the case, is a very important skill.

Spend time and learn to brief cases well—this is the time to go deep into a case. Spend all the time you need until you're sure you understand the case. The case stands for a proposition, the point of law that was decided by it, which then applies to similar cases in the same jurisdiction. By having your case brief, you can see at a glance what the case determined factually, the legal point on which the decision turned, and the case's holding (which is binding on future cases under the deciding court's jurisdiction).

You need to learn to brief cases for many reasons: (1) the case briefs may be necessary as a starting point for class discussion; (2) to be able to analyze them for your understanding of how law is created; (3) as a shorthand way of describing certain rules of law (e.g., a woman has the right to have an abortion in the first trimester of pregnancy—*Roe v. Wade*); and (4) as a way to practice a skill needed in real law practice after law school, a skill that's tested in the performance exam portion of the bar examination.

It took me a long time to brief my first cases, but with more experience, it goes faster and faster. There's no substitute for this practice (not to mention that it is a key in most law practice as well).

It is best not to buy books with canned briefs, although you could use them to check your understanding, completeness, and accuracy. If you do use canned briefs, be disciplined. Don't use them in lieu of learning the skill of briefing cases, which is important. **Learn to do it right.** Moreover, briefing cases is excellent practice for the Performance Exam portions of the Bar Exam (see page 50). Don't slow down your progress by excess haste in this important area. It will only come back to haunt you later.

case briefing

<u>Topic:</u>	e.g.—Mental State for Crime of Murder
<u>Case Name/Year:</u>	e.g.—*Delaney v. Baker* (1999)
<u>Parties:</u>	Who are the parties? Who is the plaintiff/ defendant/ appellant/ appellee?
<u>Court:</u>	Who filed where? Which court are we in? State/federal, etc?
<u>Issue:</u>	What is the issue on appeal?
<u>Analysis:</u>	What is the Analysis or Rationale used?
<u>Rule:</u>	What is the rule of law?
<u>Dissenting Opinion:</u>	What did the dissenting opinion state?
<u>Concurring Opinion:</u>	What did the concurring opinion state? (if applicable)
<u>VIP Question:</u>	Don't forget a final question—what do *you* think? Did the court reach a correct result in *your* opinion?

the IRAC method

Most law students practice writing case briefs as well as essays using some variation of the IRAC method.

I	Issue	What is the issue on which the court decision turned?
R	Rule	What is the rule of law the court formulated?
A	Application Analysis	How did the court go about reaching its decision?
C	Conclusion	What was the conclusion in the case?

Learn to carefully define the **issue** of a case on appeal, spot the **rule**, and then the **application** or **analysis** from the Court to its **conclusion**. (See the case brief headings on the previous diagram.)

During an essay exam, you basically perform the same analysis as the courts do in a case brief; you're spotting the issue, giving the rule or elements of the cause of action, then applying the facts to the law, and reaching a conclusion.

listen to lectures on tape or CD

This is how to make the minutes count—listen to tapes or CDs everywhere: in the car, in the shower, or while cooking dinner for the kids. Just promise yourself you will really listen.

HOW❂TIP

when listening to tapes or CDs: just listen!

If you don't pay attention and are daydreaming—STOP! Rewind and refocus. During long drives, reward yourself with some rock & roll (or whatever helps you to refresh your mind) after one side of each lecture tape or CD section. As Winston Churchill said: *"Change is the master key. The tired parts of the mind can be rested and strengthened not merely by rest but by using other parts."*

hands-on experience

A challenge for many law students is that in some classes there's little that relates to their life experience. Even if you are a paralegal or this is your second career, there will be areas of law you have never dealt with. With so much knowledge to assimilate, it can be hard to figure out what is really going on because it may seem too theoretical.

Law is ultimately practical. Every course should therefore really "connect." It's a good idea to have some direct, personal, hands-on experience with each subject of study whenever possible.

In my first year of law school, while working as an investigator, I was wrongfully sued in relation to a major art fraud investigation I conducted. After prevailing in court, I successfully sued two attorneys for abuse of process and malicious prosecution (so as not to have their baseless allegations affect my moral character determination) in pro per (representing myself) in San Francisco County Superior Court.

In the process, I learned more about these two tort causes of action than ever would be required for any law school exam or bar exam, and the experience of doing legal research on my own actual cases, propounding discovery, taking depositions, and going to court was invaluable.

make the law come alive for yourself!

- Go to Court and attend part of a "Law and Motion" session of the Court.

- Witness part of a criminal or civil trial—see the rules of evidence in action (not just on television).

- Study an actual contract you have signed (perhaps without having read it fully).

- Review your actual rental agreement or mortgage documents.

- Go to the law library and look at a copy of the Federal Register.

- Read an actual will or trust document.

- Talk to a lawyer or a private investigator.

- Take a summer job in a law office (apply as early as possible)

certified law student program

Another hands-on experience that's available in many jurisdictions is the Certified Law Student Program. A certified law student may perform actual lawyer tasks under the supervision of an experienced lawyer. Some activities such as taking depositions or court appearances and trials have to take place under direct personal supervision of the supervising attorney.

In California, the State Bar grants applications and monitors the requirements. You have to be at least in your second year of law school, in good standing, and actively enrolled with passing grades in courses of civil procedure and evidence.

I applied to become a certified law student as early as possible and was able to make court appearances, take depositions, and negotiate settlements. This was again a terrific practical learning experience. For more information, see the California State Bar website, www.calbar.ca.gov.

other useful study aids
flashcards

Flashcards are particularly useful. They are handy for memorizing and testing materials because you can take them with you anywhere you go. You can make your own, but there are commercial flashcards on the market as well, such as *Law in a Flash* published by Emanuel, either on actual flash cards or on CD-ROM (recommended because it is easy and fun to use and you can mark the flashcards you need to repeat and you can print them out too).

Flash cards are useful because they teach in question format the most essential parts of each course. You can and should take them with you wherever you go. You can add to the flashcards when you have more information you want to memorize. Build your flashcard review into your daily schedule.

CueCard is a simple and intuitive flash card program that you can download for free at www.download.com. Just make up cards for what you want to memorize, and

CueCard will quiz you on them. CueCard features smart testing and printing as well.

Front of Flashcard

Elements of Burglary

Back of Flashcard

- Breaking
- Entering
- Dwelling House
- Of Another
- In the Night Time (1/2 hour after sunset until 1/2 hour before sunrise)
- With Intent to Steal or Commit a Dangerous Felony Therein

*modernly, the requirements of dwelling house and nighttime are often eliminated.

sign up at <u>www.findlaw.com</u> for legal columns of interest that will be e-mailed to you at no charge on a daily or weekly basis

STUDY PHASE II
exam preparation

Aristotle advised that we learn by doing. There's no field of endeavor where that's more true than in the study of law.

> ## the best way to prepare for exams is to take exams

After your coursework, now is the time to practice under real-life exam conditions; write essays, practice MBEs (multistate bar examination multiple choice questions), time them, and have your tests graded.

Start the second phase as early as possible. Don't try to know everything perfectly before you start to practice exam taking; you're still adding to and sharpening your knowledge of the rules of law, as well as honing your analytical skills, and your issue spotting technique. Mastery of exam taking technique takes considerable time; this is why you should start the second phase as early as possible.

essays, MBEs, and performance exams

The bar examination consists of three types of exams. Most law schools follow these three types for their midterm and final exams:

1. <u>Essays</u>: In your essays, you're demonstrating your legal knowledge and your careful reading, writing, analytical thinking, and reasoning skills. In an essay examination, you're given a hypothetical fact pattern, which you have to analyze according to the call of the question, the actual instruction at the bottom of the essay requesting you to discuss some or all issues raised. This means that you have to

spot what legal issues are being raised by the facts, describe the law applicable to the facts at issue, and then analyze how a finder-of-fact would come to a conclusion in this particular situation. This is known as applying the law to the facts.

2. <u>MBEs</u>: The MBEs (Multistate Bar Exam—multiple choice questions with four answer possibilities) test fine distinctions in law, as well as analysis, reasoning, and reading comprehension.

3. <u>Performance Exams</u>: The third type of examination is the performance exam, which tests actual lawyering skills and abilities a first-year attorney needs to possess. In a performance exam, the applicant is given a memorandum outlining one or more tasks. A small "library" of cases and statutes that may or may not be applicable and a "file" of letters, memos, interview notes, etc., are what you have to base your assignment on.

1. essay examinations

Most law students will do anything but practice essay writing; it's such a demanding and active learning process. But if you want to succeed, don't have mercy on yourself!

HOW❷TIP

TIP for success:
write one essay each and every day

There are two ways of practicing essay-writing skills: *unlimited time 'open book' practice* and *timed practice*.

unlimited time 'open book' practice

Take as long as you need to look up substantive law and review notes. This is useful for the first few essays on each subject, so that you get a feeling for what it's all about. It's also useful when you're not yet skilled in the essay writing technique or lack knowledge of the substantive material.

timed practice

Timed practice, the second way of practicing essay exam writing, is a timed session allowing exactly the same time you will have under actual exam conditions without the opportunity to review any materials or notes.

There's no substitute for writing lots of timed essay exams and having them reviewed and graded. *Practice makes perfect* and writing *timed* essays is a must. Practice under the same time pressure as during your finals or during the bar exam. You have only one hour for each essay exam. This leads to a very important fact: each hour is only 60 minutes long during bar exams: there's no time for coffee breaks, although you may step out to use the restroom, have a drink of water, etc.

under-here-therefore method

An excellent method for essay writing is the *Under-Here-Therefore* approach.

Professor Tim Tyler, Ph.D., has written an excellent series called *Nailing the Bar*, focusing exclusively on the *Under-Here-Therefore* method. See www.lawtutor.org or www.americaslegalbookstore.com for more information.

The California State Bar Committee of Bar Examiners publishes model answers that frequently follow this solid approach. See www.calbar.org.

With this approach, you start your analysis of the hypothetical examination always with an issue question, followed by three paragraphs starting with *Under, Here,* and *Therefore*. You will be asked in the call of the exam question what the rights of some or all of the parties are; whether or not A or B are guilty of a crime or of some specific crime like murder; whether nephew will have an enforceable contract with uncle; if A sues B for negligence, will she recover; etc. Several logical steps are required to analyze the hypothetical. You must describe these steps in clear order and do your analysis without jumping to unsupported conclusions.

For example, don't write: "*Clearly A is guilty of manslaughter because there was mitigation from murder to manslaughter.*" Or, "*Obviously, there was no valid contract, so A has no obligations at all.*" This is conclusion only and not worth much point value on an exam. To come to any conclusion, right or wrong, there needs to be a proper analysis of the facts.

Example 1:

Issue—Does the Uniform Commercial Code (UCC) Apply to the Sale of the Chainsaw?

Under contract law the UCC applies to all transactions in goods. Goods are defined as chattels, movable at the time of the transaction.

Here, the transaction is a sale of chainsaws from Norman Bates to Edwards Scissorhands. Chainsaws are movable chattels and thus are considered goods under the UCC.

Therefore, the UCC is applicable to this transaction.

Example 2:

Issue—Was a Burglary Committed?

Under Criminal Law, burglary consists of the following elements: a breaking, an entering, of the dwelling place, of another, in the nighttime, with the intent to commit a felony therein.

Here, Dave broke the window in order to enter the door. Thus a breaking was committed.

Here, Dave entered through the door, thus there was an entry.

Here, Dave entered the garage, which isn't normally considered a dwelling house. We're not informed if the garage was attached to the dwelling house. Modernly the requirement of a dwelling house is often eliminated.

Here, the garage belonged to Victor, therefore the element "of another" was satisfied.

Here, Dave stole a 62 Corvette, according to the plan, and thus had the intent to commit a felony (theft).

Therefore, modernly Dave would be guilty of burglary. Under common law, it depends if the garage was attached to the dwelling house.

By consistently using the *Under-Here-Therefore* approach, you create a proven track to run on and don't need to search for connector words to phrase your sentence. You will never forget to mention what law applies—using *Under*; you will never jump to conclusions—using *Here* (which is where you analyze); and you will never forget to draw a conclusion—using *Therefore*.

Note that you should start with a statement of the issue followed by a question mark. Don't simply state: Issue—UCC or Issue—Burglary. This tells the exam grader nothing, and you still have to write a sentence to inform the exam grader what the actual issue is.

While the *Under-Here-Therefore* approach isn't the only one, it's a good starting point. Once you're fully familiar with what to discuss and how, you can take small liberties.

outline your answer

Outlining your essay exam is a must. Force yourself to spend 10 to 15 minutes outlining the answer. Don't skip this part, however tempting. Read the call of the question first. Then read the exam hypothetical two times. **Consider that each fact is probably important and means something. THINK. Then spend 45 to 50 minutes typing or writing as efficiently as possible. Try to leave two minutes for spell checking, underlining, and final review.**

There's almost never time enough to do it perfectly. Work fast, work smart, and stick to the outline, on which you mark how much writing time you will give to each issue (depending on their importance and complexity—major issue or sub-issue, etc.).

Here, all of the definitions and elements come in handy: having them hardwired by memorization, **now is the time** to apply them. After writing an exam essay, spend the remaining time reviewing what issues you missed: each issue counts for point value on an exam.

For example, an essay question may ask you to list all the torts and defenses that A and B can sue each other for. You may find that A can sue B for: (1) Negligence (2) Trespass to Land (3) Trespass to Chattel (4) Battery; and B can sue A for (5) Intentional Infliction of Emotional Distress and (6) Defamation.

In this example, you have six issues to write on. You may determine that there's no negligence because the element of duty isn't met and that this will be a very short discussion (you allocate 2-5 minutes). On the other hand, perhaps there's a complicated set of facts determining whether or not the defense of private necessity is applicable to the trespass to land issue (you may wish to allocate 10 minutes), and you have to discuss whether there's a valid defense of defense of property to the battery cause of action (allocate perhaps 7-10 minutes). And so on.

In the margin, mark how you're going to divide your 45 to 50 minutes for writing on these subjects. Otherwise, you will run out of time and miss points for not writing on the last issue, in this case, defamation.

think defenses and remedies

Think Defenses and Remedies. By remembering this simple rule for essay exams, I tried not to miss major issues, since I would often forget both. There's lots of point value in fully analyzing that a defendant, who may be liable for a tort or guilty of a crime, may have an arguable defense or that the logical conclusion of any issue may be an analysis of what the person may ultimately recover.

HOW❷TIP

---

in essay exams:
think defenses and remedies

discuss related concepts

Several exam issues are often related, so it pays off thinking of them in pairs or groups. When discussing defamation, consider invasion of privacy, which is often appropriate; when discussing assault, discuss battery. For each course, make a list of such possible pairs or groups. You will clearly see these after taking half a dozen practice exams.

wear the right 'hat'

There are certain 'hats' to wear during exams. In criminal law, try to be a prosecutor: find as many crimes as possible. In criminal procedure, be a defense attorney: find as many reasons why the search or seizure is illegal. Your favorite 'hat' should be that of the *top issue spotter*, the person that spots most, if not all, of the issues on each exam.

Don't take this to extremes. Be neutral and don't let yourself be swept away by ideology or emotions. (On the MBE, there are usually a few questions where your emotions will make you want to find someone guilty or not—don't fall into this trap.) Keep defenses and remedies in mind. Don't be pro-plaintiff or pro-defendant. This isn't the time to show you're for or against tort reform, for example.

how to practice issue spotting

When you feel you have truly mastered a style of writing and analysis, such as the *Under-Here-Therefore* method, and have practiced and written several hundred essays, you may feel you simply want to speed matters up and do issue spotting only.

In issue spotting, you simply write your outline during the first 12 to 15 minutes. Then you review a model answer to see if you missed any issues. This is very good practice before the bar examination because your time will be very limited and you'll want to review as much testing material as possible.

criticize yourself honestly and actively

How can I write more concisely? Do I miss major issues? Do I miss sub-issues? How are my definitions—do I miss elements? Am I spending too much time on introductions, history lessons, and side issues? Do I provide enough argument?

have your essays reviewed and graded

Have your essays reviewed by a professor, or a tutor, or another student, and be open to criticism. It's best to get feedback from several different sources.

My good friend, attorney Robert Fruitman, suggested getting my essays critiqued and graded by "*someone who doesn't like you very much…*" This advice was invaluable. Flattery doesn't get you anywhere!

HOW❂TIP

> ## get your essays graded by someone… someone who doesn't like you very much!

If your handwriting is bad, type the exams—no excuses unless you can't type fast enough. You need to be able to type with a speed of at least 30 words per minute to make it worth typing the exam. Typed exams are almost always more legible and thus more reader-friendly for the grader.

In California, at both the baby bar and general bar examination, you're allowed to type your exams.

Use the one-page outline that you have memorized in your mind—each exam tests one or more areas of the outline. By writing many exams, it will become obvious where you need to study more. Take your time to review the substantive course materials where needed.

sources for essay exams and sample answers

- State Bar Website: www.calbar.ca.gov
- *Nailing the Bar* series by Professor Tim Tyler; available at www.americaslegalbookstore.com
- Siegel Series – Essay & Multiple Choice Q & As

- Fleming's *Essay Examination Workbooks I, II, III, IV* and *Sailing through Law School Tape and CD series*
- www.findlaw.com/lawstudent go to: Bar Preparation: Essay Questions and Answers

2. MBE - the war of increments

The nationally administered MBE, created by the National Conference of Bar Examiners, covers the following six subjects:

1. **Torts**
2. **Contracts/UCC (Uniform Commercial Code)**
3. **Real Property**
4. **Criminal Law and Criminal Procedure**
5. **Evidence**
6. **Constitutional Law.**

Not all topics are MBE topics on the bar exam. In the near future, Civil Procedure will probably be added to the MBE.

The MBE part of the bar exam consists of 200 MBE questions. This breaks down as follows for practical purposes:

MBE chart

100 questions in 3 hours	The MBE portion of the Bar Exam is split into two three-hour sessions.
34 questions per hour	Or
17 questions every 30 minutes	Or
1.8 minutes per MBE question	= time pressure!

Like essay writing, practice MBE questions in a timed format, so you will be used to the time pressure that will occur during actual examinations. It's best to practice MBE questions in 30-minute increments.

Afterwards, review <u>all</u> the answers and <u>all</u> the explanations to <u>all</u> the questions. Review the correct answers as well—maybe you just made a lucky guess. **Be tough on yourself, but watch how you improve. Keeping track of your progress is the best motivator.**

Highlight the questions that you don't understand, copy them to your flashcards, and sort them by subject; every MBE question *necessarily* falls under a subject somewhere on your one-page course outline. Use these cards to review the questions you don't understand. Patterns emerge quickly. It becomes clear what subjects need more study and attention.

For example, in criminal law, I realized that questions dealing with general and specific intent caused me problems. Knowing my weaknesses and gaps in understanding made it such that I could do something about them. Make a note of areas you need to study more in depth, and then attack that area.

There's no substitute for doing a large number of MBEs—do lots of them, do *thousands*. This is the only way to ensure that many of the questions will be familiar on the bar exam, because you will have reviewed most of the possible issues that can come up. Truly, this is a war of increments.

sources for MBE questions

There are many good sources for MBE questions on each topic. The best MBE questions, in my opinion, are from *Strategies & Tactics for the MBE* and the *Finz Multistate Method*, because these questions have the best explanations and are most representative of the real bar exam questions.

You can buy all these good books from a good legal bookstore such as America's Legal Bookstores (<u>www.americaslegalbookstore.com</u>). I bought all my books from them. They have an 800-number (1-800-359-8010) and ship promptly.

3. performance examinations

Aperformance exam is an assignment testing lawyer skills a first-year attorney fresh out of law school should possess at a minimum. The emphasis isn't on knowing the law but on analytical and writing skills. To do a good job, you will also need to think logically and be organized.

You're given a series of documents:

1.   A memorandum or assignment page with instructions. It will be directed to Applicant and will often look like a memo from a senior partner.

2.   Files such as you find in a law office: memos, police reports, interview transcripts, notes, etc. In other words, the facts and evidence.

3.   The library, which usually consists of some cases and statutes. This library is the *law* you will use.

Unlike essay examinations, where all facts are usually important, performance examinations contain irrelevant and unimportant facts. In the performance examination files, just like in real law office files, there will be irrelevant facts. In the library, just like in any law library, some cases may be on point, some not; some contain dicta, some not, etc. A major requirement is that you're able to distinguish relevant from irrelevant facts and applicable law from inapplicable law.

Typically, a performance exam lasts either 1.5 hours or 3 hours. You will need approximately half of this time to read through the entire file and library. Do a highly abbreviated case brief of the legal decisions, and note the facts you think are important. Then put the assignment in the requested format. If a letter to a client is requested, write a letter addressed to the client. If the applicant is requested to write a legal memo to a senior partner, write a legal memo addressed to the senior partner.

There's a somewhat unpredictable element to the performance exams because the topics are wide-ranging and only general knowledge of the law is required. Your library portion of the materials will have all the cases, code sections, or statutes you will need to apply. Still, practicing a fair number of these tests is very useful.

Although the three hours to complete the exam may seem a lot at first, time will fly by; and again, outlining is critical.

sources for performance examinations

Sample performance exams from prior bar examinations with model answers are available on the State Bar website, www.calbar.ca.gov. Do them all and review your own work. The performance tests count for approximately 25% of the total bar score.

HOW❷TIP

PERFORMANCE EXAMINATION

USE OF YOUR TIME DURING THE 3-HOUR EXAM:

1 Hour	Reading and Note Taking
½ Hour	Outlining Your Answer
1 ½ Hour	Writing Exam

TOTAL 3 HOURS

---

law school examinations

Depending on your law school, the law school essay exams may follow the one-hour bar exam format. Some schools have unlimited time open book midterms. In that case, there's no reason not to have a good grade. Take all the time you need, and see how this exam reveals the gaps in your knowledge.

Finals in law school presume that you have mastered the entire course. You should by then have finished your entire casebook, briefed all the required cases, created your outline, and practiced taking timed exams. As you will see, your careful planning will have paid off.

baby bar examination

In California, if you don't attend an ABA approved or California accredited law school, you have to take the First-Year Law Students' Examination (FYLSX), also called the Baby Bar. Additionally, students who have not completed at least two years of college prior to matriculating at ABA approved and California accredited law schools are required to take and pass the FYLSX. This is a full day exam: 4 essays and 100 MBE questions. The subjects are contracts, torts, and criminal law (but not criminal procedure). The subjects are evenly distributed over the MBE portion of the exam, but there will be two tort or two contract essay questions and only one criminal law essay question.

The name "Baby Bar" is deceptive. The required mastery of the subjects is identical to the requirements for the General Bar Exam. "Baby" just means it is a one-day exam instead of a three-day exam.

Studying for the Baby Bar really got me into good study habits for the rest of my four-year program and forced me early on to practice the exam writing and the techniques detailed here.

Here is my personal Baby (Bar) story. The night before taking the Baby Bar, I stayed over at the home of my brother Peter and my sister-in-law Vittoria in the Bay Area. This was as close as I could get to the test center. I was sleeping in the guestroom next to my little nephew Rocky, then a little baby. Just as I was ready to doze off, he started snoring! Loudly! It was hard to believe a little baby could make so much noise and that my other nephew, Sean, didn't wake up. I didn't close an eye that night. The moral of the story is to get a good night's rest the *second night* before the exam. And it may be smart to stay in a hotel the night before. Of course, there are always double espressos...

For more information and sample essay questions, see www.calbar.ca.gov, and go to the First-Year Law Students' Examination (FYLSX) page. The National Conference of Bar Examiners designs the MBE questions (see www.ncbex.org) for the FYLSX. The NCBE sells sample MBE booklets with representative questions. Unfortunately, they don't provide explanations.

You can take the Baby Bar even
if you're not required to do so.
This is very beneficial preparation
for the general bar examination.

MPRE —
Multistate Professional Responsibility Examination

In addition to passing the bar exam, you must also register with the National Conference of Bar Examiners and pass a 50-question multistate examination on professional responsibility and conduct. In California, a scaled score of 79 is required to pass; other jurisdictions have different minimum score requirements.

You may take the MPRE after your first year of law school, but it makes sense to wait until you have taken and passed the course in professional responsibility.

This may well be the only test where you will have sufficient time to complete it. In fact, almost everyone taking it finishes early and well before the two hours and five minutes for the exam have passed. When I took it, I was the last one to leave the examination room.

For more information and sample tests, go to www.ncbex.org.

HOW I PREPARED FOR THE CALIFORNIA GENERAL BAR EXAM AND PASSED

The California General Bar Exam is a three-day test, administered each year in February and July. Look on the State Bar website (www.calbar.ca.gov) for more information and past bar exams. Signing up takes place well in advance, and if you want to use your laptop with word processor or typewriter, you must register early. See "A Note on Computer Use" on page 60.

Day 1 and Day 3 start in the morning with three essays, followed by a performance exam in the afternoon. Day 2 is the MBE, administered nationally: 100 questions in the morning (3 hours), 100 questions in the afternoon (3 hours).

	Day 1	Day 2	Day 3
3 hours—AM	3 Essays	100 MBE	3 Essays
3 hours—PM	1 Perf. Exam	100 MBE	1 Perf. Exam

The California bar exam requires special preparation. It's generally regarded as the most difficult bar exam in the United States with the lowest pass rate in the nation. There are so many areas the examiners can question you on and in so much depth that it is difficult to be fully prepared. It's therefore critical to have a good and efficient study method.

I started serious bar exam preparation seven months before the July bar exam. During these seven months, I focused on MBE practice on a daily basis (doing 17, 34, or 50 MBE questions each day) as well as on a substantive review of the 14 bar subjects in areas I felt weak in.

During the exam, time roars by and every minute is to be used, so it is hard to take a step back and be objective about how you're performing. It is, however, a great feeling to complete the exam and to have given it 100% or more of your best effort. I had decided in advance I was going to do just that.

> # decide in advance you will give it 100% or more !!!

During the last critical months, I didn't take a substantive bar review course. I had taken and completed one before then. Instead, I practiced exam taking under timed conditions only. I felt I couldn't spare the time listening to someone else's lectures when I could be doing what I really needed to be doing most urgently—taking sample examinations. Once a week, a law tutor criticized and graded some of my essays and performance tests. Getting critical feedback on essays is extremely useful.

Fortunately, I could take the entire month of July off (thanks to my good friend and boss, attorney Abe Goldman) to give my studies a final push. Perhaps two months would have been even better, but this wasn't possible, and also, in hindsight, I wouldn't have studied with the same intensity during the final weeks. I realized that the last six months building up to the bar exam with the MBE practice and substantive review were very important.

I was also very lucky to stay at the house of a good friend in Los Angeles to "housesit" for one full month (thanks Gino and family!), so I had a quiet space where I could study **absolutely uninterrupted** and spread out all my books, notes, and outlines all over the floors of the house. The only other thing I had to do was to water the plants—amazingly, they lived.

my schedule

(THE LAST MONTH BEFORE THE BAR EXAM)

My schedule was simple—100 MBE questions each **morning** on a specific subject; first 50 new questions, then the missed questions from earlier tests. I kept separate piles for each subject. This was always **timed** practice—34 questions in one hour followed by a short break.

In the **afternoon**, I would write two or three full essays followed by reviewing and issue spotting the answers from model answers. Sometimes, after that, I would issue spot half a dozen former bar exams. I would do all of them on a different subject each day. This is, after all, not that much time because with 14 bar subjects, I only spent about two days on each subject in the final month. This really makes you feel the time crunch you're under.

After that (by that time it was **evening**), I would do a substantive review, trying to focus on areas where I felt I didn't know the law well enough. I listened to tapes while eating, or while working out or taking a little walk, using my Walkman, and fell asleep doing some flashcards.

As I embarked on my month of seclusion, an attorney friend, Frank Mead III, gave me a good piece of advice: **Don't waste time studying what you already know. Put the other way—focus only on what you don't know yet.** All too often before then, I would be tempted to repeat tapes I had already listened to. Instead, Frank's advice now forced me to dive directly into the hardest part of each course.

<table>
<tr><td>HOW❂TIP</td><td>**don't waste time studying what you already know**

put the other way —
focus on what you do not know yet</td></tr>
</table>

Consequently, I found that listening to many of the tapes I had bought was going too slow, because a lot of the information was already assimilated. Repeating examples and introductory ideas was no longer useful. At that point, reading became the faster way to get to the new "stuff." There was plenty to choose from, and I made a special effort in those areas that I proved to be weak in (through practice exams and MBE questions).

FOCUS ON DIFFICULT AREAS IN EACH COURSE!

For example:
- Impeachment and Hearsay Exceptions in Evidence
- Future Interests, Real Covenants & Equitable Servitudes, Mortgages in Real Property
- Product Liability Theories and Defamation in Torts
- Contract Damages in the UCC
- 4th Amendment Exceptions to Warrant Requirement in Criminal Procedure.
- Federal Violations in Corporations
- Classifications Issues in Community Property
- Jurisdiction and Joinder rules in Civil Procedure
- Etc.

I'm sure the lists and outlines are somewhat different for everyone, but after sampling half a dozen exams, you know what areas may well be on the test, where you're weak and need extra practice.

poster outlines

I also made a one-page poster size outline per subject (on a large, firm piece of paper) with all the definitions and rules of law I wanted to memorize—I would review these daily. These were the charts I reviewed the last day before the exam and the morning of the exam.

MBEs

With the MBEs, I had started several months earlier, taking first 17 questions at a time, then 34, and then 50, to build up some mental endurance, and sometimes doing 100 or 200 just to get a feeling for real exam time pressure.

To keep track of how many MBEs I did, I hung a dry erase score board on the wall of my study room. I did a total of more than **6,000** MBEs from various sources. See page 49, "Sources for MBE Questions."

keep records and scorecards, and see improvement!

I would write down the answers on a separate page, not in the question book itself, so I could redo the missed questions without seeing what answer I had chosen before. With some questions, I had to do this more than three times before I remembered the right answer. It's really amazing how difficult they can make some MBE questions. And I had to look at it from the other side too and admit that there were areas where I simply didn't grasp or apply legal principles correctly.

Few things are as disappointing as having done thousands of questions and still scoring barely above 60%, which happened to me at times, but I tried hard not to be discouraged. If you build a good review strategy of the missed questions, you will get sharper and build your knowledge of the law. The MBE portion of the exam is truly a war of increments.

it's critical to learn from your mistakes and to try hard not to repeat them

(some people believe this is true in life as well as in law school)

The MBE exams focus on fine-line distinctions, so there's no substitute for doing a very large number of them. Redoing the missed questions when you no longer recall them is very useful. Wait at least a few weeks. It's said that at some point you can reach a point of diminished return. That may be true, but I admit that I didn't feel I had reached that point even after more than 6,000 questions.

Having marked the MBEs I had repeatedly missed, it was very useful to review these the days right before the exam.

On the MBE portion of the actual bar exam, I found there were quite a few "old friends," but frequently there was a slight new twist, so careful reading is an absolute must.

essays

I pulled as many past bar essay questions with model answers from the State Bar website as I could and also obtained bar exam essay books with model answers and outlines. I wrote or issue spotted approximately 15 exams in each subject area, so I did approximately 300 essay exams in the last months.

I had real trouble forcing myself to outline and issue spot for 15 minutes per question. Only after repeatedly proving to myself that it really worked could I force the change. My tendency was to start typing immediately. This is a bad habit because (and this was hard for myself to acknowledge, but true) I would still run out of time and major issues were missed. The reason was that my writing would become too verbose as I was thinking my way through the answer while writing.

The best method is to make an abbreviated outline of everything you're going to discuss, then divide the remaining 45-50 minutes between the issues you plan to discuss, and stick to the outline and time allocation, leaving a few minutes at the very end for outlining, spell checking, and a final review. See page 41, "Essay Examinations."

The bar examiners aren't interested in history, policy reasons behind the law, or lengthy explanations. The simple tactic is to hit the target issue, to analyze it, and to move on to a brief conclusion.

performance exams

There's no substantive law that's useful to study in advance here, since the law to be used will be in the exam's library (usually from the fictitious State of Columbia), so I did approximately 10 full performance exams until I felt that I got my note taking and organization somewhat under control.

The test lasts 3 hours. The first 1 to 1 ½ hours must be spent reading the file and library. Then, when you finally start writing, where are you going to find your facts or law? They have to be very accessible. The best method I found was to brief the cases using the IRAC method, writing or underlining the Issue, Rule, Application, and Conclusion directly on the library outline itself, and to write the issues of note on the file outline, so there are only three pages to look at, the instructions to the applicant being the third page.

Pay close attention to "lists" in the examination's library such as the factors a court considers in an authority, because they will become a key focus point of your writing.

Depending on the format of your assignment (write a letter to a client, write a memo to a senior partner, write a discovery plan, or write points and authorities), the tone in which you address the client, senior partner, or court is different. You will explain the matter in easy to understand language to the client, whereas you can use legalese and citations with the senior partner in the firm and the court. The pleading format should be the most formal. Reviewing some of the previous bar tests and answers gives a good idea of what to expect and how to format your writing. See page 50, "Performance Examinations."

a note on computer use (california)

I typed my exams on my laptop, since I have a hard time reading my own handwriting. You can bring a laptop, mouse, keyboard with wrist pads, earplugs, copyholder, etc. In short, there's no reason not to have a comfortable set-up with your laptop computer. You may not bring your computer case into the exam room, so leave it in your car or hotel room.

Softest software

You have to pre-register with Examsoft Software, www.examsoft.com, and download the software. The bar examiners provide you with detailed instructions after you register for the examination. I took all my practice exams on it in the last month, so I was familiar with its limited word processing capabilities.

Softest blocks all other programs on your computer while you're using it, so there's no need to delete any files from your laptop. There's a spell checker on the program that's enabled during the entire bar exam (in California).

passing the bar

Few moments in life are as exciting as logging in to the State Bar website a few days before Thanksgiving—almost four months after the examination, and following weeks of agony thinking that you couldn't possibly have passed—and then (after getting the message that the Bar's website is experiencing extremely heavy traffic and to "please be patient") finally getting the news that you're on the pass list.

And, there is no gloating here! You will never know if you barely passed by a few points or did well, so it is really a humbling experience. It's in such moments you realize you have a lot to be grateful for—and that you could have never passed the Bar without the support of your loved ones and friends.

The following Monday the State Bar oath card and other materials were already in my mailbox. I called the Judge's secretary and asked if I could come over to be sworn in right away. A new learning curve had started…

what to do if you did not pass the bar?

The difficult question is—now what? The best advice is that the basic nature of the bar examination doesn't change. On the MBE portion, it is a war of increments. On the essays and performance tests, success depends on your analytical and issue spotting skills. These two supremely important skills can be trained and thus improved with practice.

You will be provided with a detailed breakdown per subject of your essay scores and MBE results. As much as possible, narrow down and focus on areas where you need to improve and practice as many essay exams and MBEs as you can. Keep reviewing all the courses and keep building up your knowledge, just as when you studied for the bar the first time. Use the methods and techniques outlined in this guide.

Surround yourself with supportive people during law school and during exam prep time, and give yourself all the support and encouragement you need.

GOOD LUCK!

american bar association

www.abanet.org

bookstores

www.americaslegalbookstore.com
www.amazon.com
www.barnesandnoble.com
www.ababooks.org

california

judicial council of california
www.courtinfo.ca.gov

california codes
http://caselaw.lp.findlaw.com/cacodes/index.html

california code of regulations
www.calregs.com

witkin legal institute
www.witkin.com

careers

legal careers/martindale.com
www.martindale.com/xp/Martindale/Legal_Careers/careers_intro.xml

codes

united states codes
www.findlaw.com/casecode/uscodes/index.html

code of federal regulations
www.gpoaccess.gov/cfr/index.html

the college board

www.collegeboard.com

government records / records search

citizens guide to requesting records
www.fas.org/sgp/foia/citizen.html

principal foia contacts at federal agencies
www.usdoj.gov/04foia/foiacontacts.htm

your right to federal records
www.pueblo.gsa.gov/cic_text/fed_prog/foia/foia.htm

department of justice foia guide
www.usdoj.gov/oip/foi-act.htm

department of justice privacy act
www.usdoj.gov/04foia/04_7_1.html

free public records directory (limited search availability)
www.searchsystems.net

records search (subscription / free trial)
www.accurint.com

records search (subscription / some free)
www.publicdata.com

links to all federal courts

www.uscourts.gov/allinks.html

law school admission council

www.lsac.org

legal resources (check them out!)

the 'lectric law library
www.lectlaw.com

hieros gamos
www.hg.org

internet legal research group
www.ilrg.com
www.lawcentral.com
www.megalaw.com
www.lawsource.com
www.legalengine.com
www.socrateslawreview.com
www.legal.com
www.lawguru.com
www.thelawengine.com

financing law school
www.stu.findlaw.com/prelaw/finance.html

national conference of bar examiners

www.ncbex.org

association of trial lawyers of america

www.atla.org

legal research

www.findlaw.com (free!)
www.lexis.com
www.lexisnexis.com/about
www.lexisnexis.com/lawschool
www.loislaw.com
www.michie.com
www.westlaw.com

grammar and writing

online writing lab
http://owl.english.purdue.edu

the elements of style
http://sut1.sut.ac.th/strunk/index.html

guide to grammar and writing
http://ccc.commnet.edu/grammar

online english grammar
www.edufind.com/english/grammar

the grammar lady
www.grammarlady.com

dr grammar
www.drgrammar.org

the english department
http://the_english_dept.tripod.com/students.html

dave's ESL cafe
www.eslcafe.com

guide to grammar and writing
http://ccc.commnet.edu/grammar/

internet public library
www.ipc.org

guide to grammar and writing
www.ccc.commnet.edu/grammar

confusing words
www.confusingwords.com

law tutor

www.lawtutor.org

library of congress

library of congress
www.loc.gov

bill of rights
http://lcweb2.loc.gov/const/bor.html

constitution of the united states
http://lcweb2.loc.gov/const/constquery.html

law library of congress
www.loc.gov/law

software

cuecard - free computer flashcard program
www.download.com

examsoft software
www.examsoft.com

APPENDIX B
united states state bar organizations

Alabama
www.alabar.org

Alaska
www.alaskabar.org

Arizona
www.azbar.org

Arkansas
www.arkbar.com

California
www.calbar.org

Colorado
www.cobar.org

Connecticut
www.ctbar.org

Delaware
www.dsba.org

District of Columbia
www.dcbar.org

Florida
www.flabar.org

Georgia
www.gabar.org

Hawaii
www.hsba.org

Idaho
www.state.id.us/isb

Illinois
www.illinoisbar.org

Indiana
www.ai.org/isba

Iowa
www.iowabar.org

Kansas
www.ksbar.org

Kentucky
www.kybar.org

Louisiana
www.lsba.org

Maine
www.mainebar.org

Maryland
www.msba.org

Massachusetts
www.massbar.org

Michigan
www.michbar.org

Minnesota
www.mnbar.org

Mississippi
www.msbar.org

Missouri
www.mobar.org

Montana
www.montanabar.org

Nebraska
www.nebar.com

Nevada
www.nvbar.org

New Hampshire
www.nhbar.org

New Jersey
www.njsba.com

New Mexico
www.nmbar.org

New York
www.nysba.org

North Carolina
www.barlinc.org

North Dakota
www.sband.org

Ohio
www.ohiobar.org

Oklahoma
www.okbar.org

Oregon
www.osbar.org

Pennsylvania
www.pabar.org

Rhode Island
www.ribar.com

South Carolina
www.scbar.org

South Dakota
www.sdbar.org

Tennessee
www.tba.org

Texas
www.texasbar.com

Utah
www.utahbar.org

Vermont
www.vtbar.org

Virginia
www.vsb.org

Washington
www.wsba.org

West Virginia
www.wvbar.org

Wisconsin
www.wisbar.org

Wyoming
www.wyomingbar.org

ALABAMA

birmingham school of law
http://www.bsol.com

faulkner university
thomas goode jones school of law
http://www.faulkner.edu/law/

samford university
http://www.samford.edu/schools/law/index.html

university of alabama law school
http://www.law.ua.edu/

ARIZONA

arizona state university
http://www.law.asu.edu/

university of arizona
http://www.law.arizona.edu

ARKANSAS

university of arkansas, fayetteville
http://law.uark.edu

university of arkansas, little rock
http://www.ualr.edu/%7elawschool

CALIFORNIA

abraham lincoln university school of law
http://www.alu.edu/law/law.html

american college of law
http://www.aclaw.com

california pacific school of law
http://www.calpaclaw.edu

california western
http://www.cwsl.edu/

chapman university school of law
http://www.chapman.edu/law/

concord university school of law
http://www.concordlawschool.com

glendale university college of law
http://www.glendalelaw.edu

golden gate university
http://www.ggu.edu/schools/law/home.html

hastings college of law
http://www.uchastings.edu/

inland valley university
http://www.ivucol.org/

irvine university
http://www.irvineuniversity.edu/

john f. kennedy university school of law
http://www.jfku.edu/law

lincoln law school of sacramento
http://www.lincolnlaw.edu

lincoln law school of san jose
http://www.lincolnlawsj.edu

lorenzo patiño school of law
http://www.patinolawschool.com

loyola law school los angeles
http://www.lls.edu

monterey college of law
http://www.montereylaw.edu/

new college of california school of law
http://www.newcollege.edu/law/default.htm

northwestern california university
http://www.nwculaw.edu

oak brook college of law
http://www.obcl.edu/

pacific west college of law
http://www.pacificwestcollege.com/

peoples college oflaw
http://www.peoplescollegeoflaw.edu/

pepperdine university
http://law-www.pepperdine.edu/

san fernando valley college of law
http://www.sfvlaw.edu/

san francisco law school
http://www.sfls.edu

santa barbara and ventura colleges of law
http://www.santabarbaralaw.edu/index.html

santa clara university
http://www.scu.edu/law/

silicon valley university law school
http://www.svulaw.com/

southern california institute of law
http://www.lawdegree.com/

southwestern university
http://www.swlaw.edu

stanford university
http://lawschool.stanford.edu/index.shtml

thomas jefferson school of law
http://www.jeffersonlaw.edu/

trinity law school
http://www.tls.edu

university of california, berkeley - boalt hall
http://www.law.berkeley.edu/

university of california, davis
http://kinghall.ucdavis.edu/

university of california, los angeles
http://www.law.ucla.edu/

university of la verne
http://law.ulv.edu/

university of san diego
http://www.acusd.edu/~usdlaw/

university of san francisco
http://www.law.usfca.edu/

university of southern california
http://www.usc.edu/dept/law-lib/

university of the pacific
mcgeorge school of law
http://www.mcgeorge.edu/

university of west los angeles
school of law and paralegal studies
http://www.uwla.edu/law/index.html

western state university college of law
http://www.wsulaw.edu/

whittier college
http://www.law.whittier.edu/

british-american university school of law
http://www.british-american.edu/

concord law school
http://www.concordlawschool.com

COLORADA

university of colorado
http://www.colorado.edu/law/

university of denver
http://www.law.du.edu/

CONNECTICUT

quinnipiac university school of law
http://www.quinnipiac.edu/academics/law.asp?school=lw

university of connecticut
http://www.law.uconn.edu/

yale university
http://www.law.yale.edu/

DELAWARE

widener university
http://www.law.widener.edu/

DISTRICT OF COLUMBIA

american university
http://www.wcl.american.edu/

catholic university of america
http://law.edu/

george washington university
http://www.law.gwu.edu/

georgetown university
http://www.law.georgetown.edu

howard university
http://www.law.howard.edu/

university of the district of columbia david a. clarke school of law
http://64.50.166.145/

FLORIDA

barry university, orlando campus
http://www.barry.edu/law/

florida coastal school of law
http://www.fcsl.edu

florida state university
http://www.law.fsu.edu/

nova southeastern university
http://www.nsulaw.nova.edu

st. thomas university school of law
http://www.stu.edu/lawschool/index.htm

stetson university
http://www.law.stetson.edu/

university of florida
http://www.law.ufl.edu

university of miami
http://www.law.miami.edu/

GEORGIA

emory university
http://www.law.emory.edu/

georgia state university
http://law.gsu.edu/

mercer university
walter f. george school of law
http://www.law.mercer.edu

university of georgia
http://www.lawsch.uga.edu/

HAWAII

university of hawaii, manoa
http://www.hawaii.edu/law/

IDAHO

university of idaho
http://www.law.uidaho.edu/

ILLINOIS

chicago-kent college of law
http://www.kentlaw.edu/

depaul university
http://www.law.depaul.edu

loyola university, chicago
http://www.luc.edu/schools/law/

northern illinois university
http://www.niu.edu/claw/index.htm

northwestern university
http://www.law.northwestern.edu

southern illinois university
http://www.siu.edu/~lawsch/

the john marshall law school
http://www.jmls.edu/

university of chicago
http://www.law.uchicago.edu/

university of illinois
http://www.law.uiuc.edu/

INDIANA

indiana university, bloomington
http://www.law.indiana.edu/

indiana university, indianapolis
http://www.iulaw.indy.indiana.edu/

university of notre dame
http://www.nd.edu/~ndlaw/

valparaiso university
http://www.valpo.edu/law/

IOWA

drake university
http://www.law.drake.edu

university of iowa
http://www.uiowa.edu/~lawcoll/

KANSAS

university of kansas
http://www.law.ukans.edu/

washburn university
http://washburnlaw.edu/

KENTUCKY

northern kentucky university
http://www.nku.edu/~chase

university of kentucky
http://www.uky.edu/law/

university of louisville
louis d. brandeis school of law
http://www.louisville.edu/brandeislaw/

LOUISIANA

louisiana state university
http://www.lsu.edu/guests/lsulaw/

loyola university, new orleans
http://www.loyno.edu/law/

southern university law center
http://www.sulc.edu/

tulane university
http://www.law.tulane.edu/

MAINE

university of maine
http://www.law.usm.maine.edu/

MARYLAND

university of baltimore
http://www.ubalt.edu/www/law/index.html

university of maryland
http://www.law.umaryland.edu

MASSACHUSETTS

boston college
http://www.bc.edu/bc_org/avp/law/lwsch/index.ht
ml

boston university
http://web.bu.edu/law/

harvard law school
http://www.law.harvard.edu/

massachusetts school of law
http://www.mslaw.edu/

new england school of law
http://www.nesl.edu/

northeastern university
http://www.slaw.neu.edu/

southern new england school of law
http://www.snesl.edu

suffolk university
http://www.suffolk.edu/law/

western new england college
http://www.law.wnec.edu/

MICHIGAN

ave maria school of law
http://www.avemarialaw.edu

detroit college of law
http://www.dcl.edu/

thomas m. cooley law school
http://www.cooley.edu

university of detroit
http://www.law.udmercy.edu/

university of michigan
http://www.law.umich.edu/

wayne state university
http://www.law.wayne.edu/

MINNESOTA

hamline university
http://web.hamline.edu/law

university of minnesota
http://www.law.umn.edu/

university of st. thomas school of law
http://www.stthomas.edu/lawschool/

william mitchell college of law
http://www.wmitchell.edu/

MISSISSIPPI

mississippi college school of law
http://law.mc.edu

university of mississippi
http://www.olemiss.edu/depts/law_school/law-hom.html

MISSOURI

st. louis university
http://lawlib.slu.edu/

university of missouri, columbia
http://www.law.missouri.edu/

university of missouri, kansas city
http://www.law.umkc.edu/

washington university
http://www.wulaw.wustl.edu/

MONTANA

university of montana
http://www.umt.edu/law/homepage.htm

NEBRASKA

creighton university school of law
http://culaw.creighton.edu

university of nebraska
http://www.unl.edu/lawcoll/

NEVADA

university of nevada, las vegas
http://www.law.unlv.edu/

NEW HAMPSHIRE

franklin pierce law center
http://www.fplc.edu/

NEW JERSEY

rutgers university, camden
http://www-camlaw.rutgers.edu/

rutgers university, newark
http://www.rutgers-newark.rutgers.edu/law/

seton hall university
http://www.shu.edu/law/index.html

NEW MEXICO

university of new mexico
http://lawschool.unm.edu

NEW YORK

albany law school of union university
http://www.als.edu

brooklyn law school
http://www.brooklaw.edu/

city university of new york
http://web.law.cuny.edu/

columbia university
http://www.law.columbia.edu/

cornell university
http://www.lawschool.cornell.edu/

fordham law school
http://www.fordham.edu/law/home/

hofstra university
http://www.hofstra.edu/law

new york law school
http://www.nyls.edu/

new york university
http://www.law.nyu.edu/index.html

pace university
http://www.law.pace.edu/

st. john's university
http://www.stjohns.edu/law

state university of new york - buffalo
http://www.law.buffalo.edu/site/index.html

syracuse university
http://www.law.syr.edu/

touro college - jacob d. fuchsberg law center
http://www.tourolaw.edu/

yeshiva university
http://www.yu.edu/

NORTH CAROLINA

campbell university
http://webster.campbell.edu/culawsch.htm

duke university
http://www.law.duke.edu/

north carolina central university
http://www.nccu.edu/law/

university of north carolina
http://www.law.unc.edu/

wake forest university
http://www.law.wfu.edu/

NORTH DAKOTA

university of north dakota
http://www.law.und.nodak.edu/

OHIO

capital university
http://www.law.capital.edu/

case western reserve university
http://lawwww.cwru.edu/

cleveland state university
http://www.law.csuohio.edu/

**ohio northern university
claude w. pettit college of law**
http://www.law.onu.edu/

ohio state university
http://moritzlaw.osu.edu/

university of akron law school
http://www.uakron.edu/law/

university of cincinnati
http://www.law.uc.edu/

university of dayton
http://www.udayton.edu/~law/

university of toledo
http://law.utoledo.edu/

OKLAHOMA

oklahoma city university
http://www.okcu.edu/law/

university of oklahoma
http://www.law.ou.edu/

university of tulsa
http://www.utulsa.edu/law/

OREGON

lewis and clark college
northwestern school of law
http://www.lclark.edu/law/index.html

university of oregon
http://www.law.uoregon.edu/

willamette university
http://www.willamette.edu/wucl/

PENNSYLVANIA

dickinson school of law
http://www.dsl.psu.edu/

duquesne university
http://www.duq.edu/law/law.html

temple university
http://www.temple.edu/departments/lawschool/

university of pennsylvania
http://www.law.upenn.edu/

university of pittsburgh
http://www.law.pitt.edu/

villanova university
http://vls.law.vill.edu/

RHODE ISLAND

roger williams school of law
http://www.rwu.edu/law

SOUTH CAROLINA

university of south carolina
http://www.law.sc.edu/

SOUTH DAKOTA

university of south dakota
http://www.usd.edu/law/

TENNESSEE

nashville school of law
http://www.nashvilleschooloflaw.net/index.html

university of memphis
cecil c. humphreys school of law
http://www.people.memphis.edu/~law/

university of tennessee
http://www.law.utk.edu/

vanderbilt university
http://www.vanderbilt.edu/law/

TEXAS

baylor university
http://law.baylor.edu/

south texas college of law
http://www.stcl.edu/

southern methodist university
http://www.law.smu.edu/indexie.htm

st. mary's university
http://stmarylaw.stmarytx.edu

texas southern university
thurgood marshall school of law
http://www.tsulaw.edu/

texas tech university
http://www.law.ttu.edu/

texas wesleyan university school of law
http://www.law.txwes.edu

university of houston
http://www.lawlib.uh.edu/

university of texas
http://tarlton.law.utexas.edu/

UTAH

brigham young university
http://www.law.byu.edu

university of utah
http://www.law.utah.edu

VERMONT

vermont law school
http://www.vermontlaw.edu/

VIRGINIA

appalachian school of law
http://www.asl.edu/library/index.html

college of william and mary marshall whythe school of law
http://www.wm.edu/law

george mason university
http://www.gmu.edu/departments/law/

regent university school of law
http://www.regent.edu/acad/schlaw/

university of richmond
http://www.urich.edu/~law/

university of virginia
http://www.law.virginia.edu/index.htm

washington and lee university
http://www.wlu.edu/law

WASHINGTON

gonzaga university
http://law.gonzaga.edu

seattle university law school
http://www.law.seattleu.edu/

university of washington
http://www.law.washington.edu/

WEST VIRGINIA

west virginia university
http://www.wvu.edu/%7claw

WISCONSIN

marquette university
http://www.mu.edu/dept/law/index.html

university of wisconsin
http://www.law.wisc.edu

WYOMING

university of wyoming
http://www.uwyo.edu/law/law.htm

ABOUT THE AUTHOR

David Springfield, Esq. is licensed to practice in all courts in the State of California. He has experience in the field of elder abuse, health care, and art fraud litigation, including trials, bench trials, arbitrations, summary judgment motions, discovery, mediations, and appeals in both federal and state courts.

David Springfield's practice areas include general business disputes; unfair competition and unfair business practices; Section 17200 claims; art fraud litigation; medical malpractice; elder abuse; wrongful death and survivor actions; fraud and misrepresentation; sexual harassment; defamation law; malicious prosecution and abuse of process; anti-SLAPP motions; and intellectual property law.

David Springfield has worked for the law firm of Abraham N. Goldman & Associates for more than 10 years, first as an investigator and paralegal before joining the firm as an associate attorney in 2003. As an investigator and lead paralegal, he made a major contribution in obtaining more than $35 million in judgments against various co-conspirators in a major art fraud case, and a seven figure settlement in a civil rights/jail suicide case. As an investigator, David Springfield also helped ensure defense verdicts and pre-litigation resolution for several high-profile civil and criminal cases.

David Springfield obtained his B.S.L. degree in 2001 and his J.D. degree in 2003 from Northwestern California University School of Law (Sacramento, California). He passed the California Bar Examination on his first attempt and in his first year of practice took four significant cases to trial/judicial arbitration with successful outcomes. David Springfield also currently teaches law in Sacramento, California, and teaches California State Bar review, preparation, and writing skills to law students and bar applicants. He has been a guest speaker on the topic of elder abuse on several television programs in Southern California.

COMING SOON!
titles in preparation

how 2 study CD-series

How 2 Study Law—**TORTS**
How 2 Study Law—**CONTRACTS**
How 2 Study Law—**REMEDIES**
How 2 Study Law—**CRIMINAL LAW**
How 2 Study Law—**CRIMINAL PROCEDURE**
How 2 Study Law—**EVIDENCE**
How 2 Study Law—**CIVIL PROCEDURE**
How 2 Study Law—**REAL PROPERTY**
How 2 Study Law—**CONSTITUTIONAL LAW**
How 2 Study Law—**CORPORATIONS**
How 2 Study Law—**WILLS**
How 2 Study Law—**TRUSTS**
How 2 Study Law—**COMMUNITY PROPERTY**
How 2 Study Law—**PROFESSIONAL RESPONSIBILITY**

how 2 use legal experts CD-series

How 2 Use Legal Experts—**EXPERT WITNESS**

An in-depth interview with the expert witness Saul Frechtel. Saul Frechtel shares 25 years of experience, advice, and tips for depositions and trials, all through his best anecdotes. Listen to the "Voice of Experience." A "Must" for every attorney!

How 2 Use Legal Experts—**PRIVATE INVESTIGATOR**

ordering information

Visit www.how2studylaw.com for ordering information.
Subscribe to our Email News and receive regular information on new titles.
Email us at: info@how2studylaw.com.

NOTES

NOTES

NOTES

NOTES
